WE BOTH READ®

Parent's Introduction

We Both Read is the first series of books designed to invite parents and children to share the reading of a story by taking turns reading aloud. This "shared reading" innovation, which was developed in conjunction with early reading specialists, invites parents to read the more sophisticated text on the left-hand pages, while children are encouraged to read the right-hand pages, which have been written at one of three early reading levels.

Reading aloud is one of the most important activities parents can share with their child to assist their reading development. However, *We Both Read* goes beyond reading *to* a child and allows parents to share reading *with* a child. *We Both Read* is so powerful and effective because it combines two key elements in learning: "showing" (the parent reads) and "doing" (the child reads). The result is not only faster reading development for the child, but a much more enjoyable and enriching experience for both!

Most of the words used in the child's text should be familiar to them. Others can easily be sounded out. An occasional difficult word will be first introduced in the parent's text, distinguished with **bold lettering**. Pointing out these words, as you read them, will help familiarize them to your child. You may also find it helpful to read the entire book aloud yourself the first time, then invite your child to participate on the second reading. Also note that the parent's text is preceded by a "talking parent" icon: ⊖ ; and the child's text is preceded by a "talking child" icon: ☺ .

We Both Read books is a fun, easy way to encourage and help your child to read — and a wonderful way to start your child off on a lifetime of reading enjoyment!

We Both Read: About the Seasons

Use of some photographs provided by PhotoDisc (Digital Imagery © copyright 2000 PhotoDisc., Inc.). Use of other images provided by Gettyone and Corbis Images.

We Both Read® is a registered trademark of Treasure Bay, Inc.

Published by
Treasure Bay, Inc.
P.O. Box 119
Novato, CA 94948 USA

PRINTED IN SINGAPORE

Library of Congress Control Number: 00 135761

Hardcover ISBN-10: 1-891327-27-5
Hardcover ISBN-13: 978-1-891327-27-8
Paperback ISBN-10: 1-891327-28-3
Paperback ISBN-10: 978-1-891327-28-5

We Both Read® Books
Patent No. 5,957,693

Visit us online at:
www.webothread.com

PR 02/10

To see all the We Both Read books that are available,
just go online to **www.webothread.com**

Explore the mystery and wonder of the tropical rain forest! Travel around the equator to Africa, Asia, and South America discovering the world's most fascinating plant and animal life. Captivating photographs, along with compelling text, make this Level 1–2 book an exciting adventure and a great learning experience.

To Mr. Geisel—thank you.

Sindy McKay

WE BOTH READ®

About the Seasons

By Sindy McKay

TREASURE BAY

Flowers bloom on a warm **spring** morning. The sun blazes on a hot **summer** day. Leaves crackle on an **autumn** afternoon. Snowflakes fall on a cold **winter** night.

These are the sights and sounds of the **seasons.**

1

There are four **seasons**.

They are **spring**, **summer**, **autumn**, and **winter**.

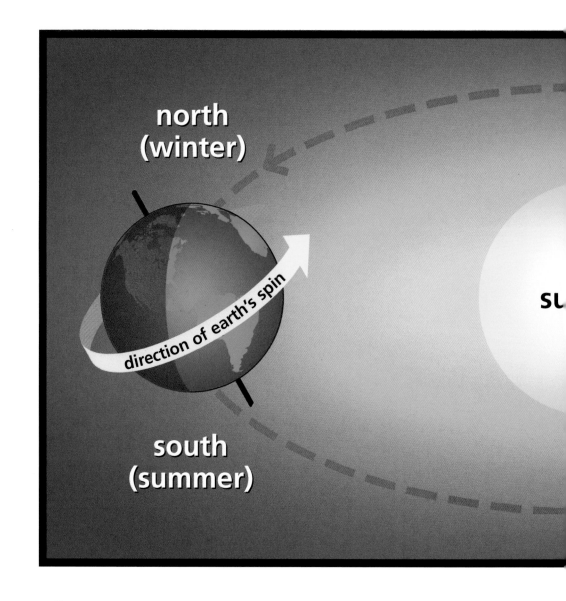

north
(winter)

direction of earth's spin

south
(summer)

su

Every year the seasons change. But do you know why? It's because the Earth is tilted!

It takes one year for the Earth to travel around the sun. For half of the year the top part of the Earth, called the Northern Hemisphere, tilts *toward* the sun.

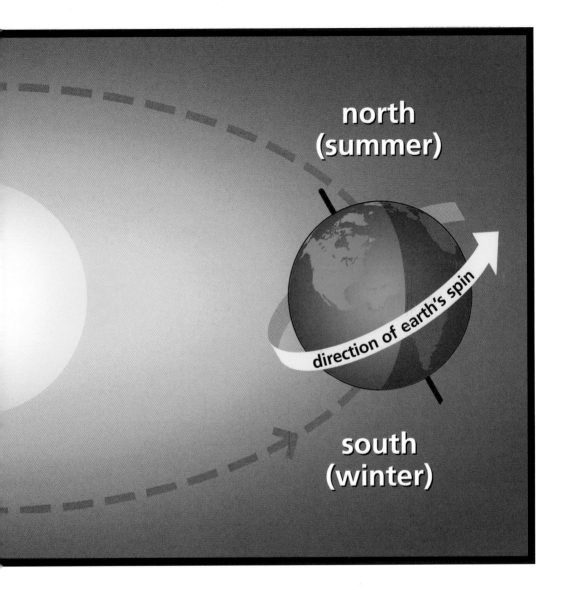

north
(summer)

direction of earth's spin

south
(winter)

That is when we have spring and summer.

   For the other half of the year, the Northern Hemisphere tilts *away* from the sun. That's when we have autumn and winter.

It's just the opposite in the Southern Hemisphere. When we are having autumn and winter, the Southern Hemisphere's having spring and summer!

 We are cold in the snow. Other kids are hot in the sun.

🌐 In the Northern Hemisphere, the summer season begins around June 21st. This date is called the summer solstice. On this day the sun shines longer than on any other day of the year.

The days are long in the summer.

There is more time to play!

   Whether swimming in a pool, frolicking in the ocean, or racing through the sprinklers in their own backyard, everyone loves to get wet in the summer.

The water is cold.
It feels good when
you are hot.

 Some foods just taste better in the summertime. Ripe, juicy watermelon is especially good on a hot, muggy summer day.

Ice cream is good, too.

It is even better when you share it.

 Just when you think you can't stand another day of heat, dark clouds roll in and a summer storm arrives to cool things down.

Summer storms can be spectacular, with dazzling streaks of lightning and deafening roars of thunder.

13

The rain stops.

A rainbow comes out.

The rainbow is full of colors.

Somewhere near the middle of September you may begin to notice that the days are getting shorter and the **leaves** on the trees are beginning to change colors. Autumn is on its way.

The **leaves** fall off the trees.

That is why autumn is also called "fall".

 Autumn officially begins on the day
of the autumnal equinox, usually around
September 21st. Equinox means "equal
night" in Latin, and on this date night and
day are equal lengths.

There is lots of wind in the fall.

It is a great time to fly a kite.

 Traditionally autumn signals the last harvest of the year. People used to have to work very hard to store up enough **food** to last through the long, cold winter.

Today we can just go to the store and buy our food in the winter.

It is fun to pick your own **food**.

This food grows very big!

 Most kids head back to **school** in the fall.

School is a wonderful place to learn about the world around us. And it's a great place to have fun and make lots of new friends.

Some kids walk to **school**.

Some kids take the bus to school.

By now the earth is halfway through its trip around the sun and we arrive at the winter solstice. On this day, around December 21st, our Northern Hemisphere no longer tilts *toward* the sun, it tilts *away* from it.

The winter season is here.

 Most places get snow in the winter.

Snow can be a lot of fun!

The day of the winter solstice is the shortest day of the year. It's the perfect day to stay inside by a cozy fire and read your favorite book.

The days are short in the winter.

But there is time to play outside.

There are many fun sports and games that can be played during the winter season. Some favorite winter activities include skiing, sledding, bobsledding, ice hockey, and building giant snowmen!

It is fun to skate on the ice.

It is also cold!

   Not every place in the Northern Hemisphere gets snow during the winter. In some places, such as Hawaii and Mexico, it stays **warm** all year long—even in the winter.

Kids do not care if it is **warm** or cold.

They just like to play.

 As much fun as winter can be, by mid-March most of us are ready for the sun to start shining again. On around March 21st, the Vernal Equinox marks the beginning of another season, as once again day and night are equal lengths.

The sun shines.

The snow melts.

It is spring again.

⎅   Many people can't wait to get outside and dig into the earth on a bright spring morning. Spring is a time for **plant**ing seeds and encouraging flowers to bloom in the warm sunshine.

 **Plants** need rain to grow.

It rains a lot in the spring.

 Plants aren't the only things that grow in the spring. Animals do, too! Every spring a brand new crop of baby animals is born.

 This is a baby deer.

A baby deer is called a fawn.

Many birds build their **nests** in the spring. It can take hundreds of trips to gather the materials needed to build them. Once built, the mother birds lay their **eggs** in the **nests** and wait for them to **hatch**. This usually takes between two and four weeks.

The **nest** keeps the **eggs** warm.

The eggs **hatch**.

Then the nest is a home for the baby birds.

Every season is filled with its own special wonders. And every year we can count on the seasons changing, bringing beauty and joy into our lives.

 Summer.

Autumn.

Winter.

Spring.

The four seasons.

40

If you liked
About the Seasons, **here are two other**
We Both Read™ **Books you are sure to enjoy!**

A very whimsical tale of a boy and his dog and their fantastic dreamland adventures. This delightful tale features fun and easy to read text for the very beginning reader, such as "pigs that dig", "fish on a dish", and a "dog on a frog." Both children and their parents will love this newest addition to the We Both Read series!